*Profiles of the Presidents*

# GEORGE
# HERBERT
# WALKER
# BUSH

★  ★  ★

*Profiles of the Presidents*

# GEORGE HERBERT WALKER BUSH

*by Marc Davis*

Content Adviser: Warren Finch, Supervisor of Archivists, George Bush Library and Museum, College Station, Texas

Reading Adviser: Dr. Linda D. Labbo, Department of Reading Education, College of Education, The University of Georgia

COMPASS POINT BOOKS ✦ MINNEAPOLIS, MINNESOTA

Compass Point Books
3722 West 50th Street, #115
Minneapolis, MN 55410

Visit Compass Point Books on the Internet at *www.compasspointbooks.com*
or e-mail your request to *custserv@compasspointbooks.com*

Photographs ©: Hulton/Archive by Getty Images, cover, 3, 24, 25, 27, 28, 29 (top), 31, 34, 40, 43, 47, 56 (bottom left & right), 57 (top left), 58 (left); Courtesy Ronald Reagan Library, 6; George Bush Presidential Library, 7, 9, 10, 13, 14, 15, 16, 17, 19, 32, 38, 42, 54 (left), 55 (left); Jana Birchum/ Getty Images, 8; Judy Griesedieck/Corbis, 11; Corbis, 12, 45; Bettmann/Corbis, 18, 20, 21, 22, 26, 33, 35, 36, 56 (top left); Wally McNamee/Corbis, 23, 29 (bottom); Reuters NewMedia Inc./Corbis, 39, 57 (bottom left), 59 (top right); AFP/Corbis, 41; Natalie Fobes/Corbis, 46; David & Peter Turnley/Corbis, 48, 58 (right); Paul S. Howell/Getty Images, 50; E. O. Hoppe/Corbis, 54 (right); Franklin D. Roosevelt Library, 55 (top right); Galen Rowell/Corbis, 55 (bottom right); NASA, 57 (right); DigitalVision, 59 (bottom right).

Editors: E. Russell Primm, Emily J. Dolbear, Melissa McDaniel, and Catherine Neitge
Photo Researcher: Svetlana Zhurkina
Photo Selector: Linda S. Koutris
Designer: The Design Lab
Cartographer: XNR Productions, Inc.

Library of Congress Cataloging-in-Publication Data

Davis, Marc, 1934–
  George Herbert Walker Bush / by Marc Davis.
     v. cm. — (Profiles of the presidents)
Includes bibliographical references and index.
Contents: A lifetime of service—The early years—Family and business matters—Mr. Bush goes to Washington—The path to the vice presidency—President George H. W. Bush—The Bush legacy.
  ISBN 0-7565-0285-3
  1. Bush, George, 1924– —Juvenile literature. 2. United States—Politics and government—1981–1989—Juvenile literature. 3. United States—Politics and government—1989–1993—Juvenile literature. 4. Presidents—United States—Biography—Juvenile literature. [1. Bush, George, 1924–2. Presidents.] I. Title. II. Series.
  E882 .D38 2002
  973.928'092—dc21                                             2002003015

# Table of Contents

★ ★ ★

# A Lifetime of Service

★　★　★

*Vice President George Herbert Walker Bush and President Ronald Reagan (left)*

**W**hen George Herbert Walker Bush ran for president of the United States in 1988, he had been vice president for eight years. Even before he became vice president, Bush had enjoyed a long career in government. Twice he had been elected to the U.S. Congress from Texas. He had also served as U.S. **ambassador** to the United Nations, as the top U.S. official in China, and as

6

director of the Central Intelligence Agency (CIA).

Before he entered government, Bush was a successful businessman. During World War II (1939–1945), he was the youngest fighter pilot in the U.S. Navy. He won a medal for bravery.

With this varied background and experience, Bush was a strong **candidate** for president. He also had the good luck to serve as

▲ *President Bush and first lady Barbara Bush after his 1989 inauguration*

vice president under Ronald Reagan, one of the nation's most popular presidents. So George Bush easily won the election in November 1988, becoming the forty-first president of the United States.

In his first speech as president, Bush said the goal of his presidency would be "to make kinder the face of the nation and gentler the face of the world." This statement set the tone for Bush's presidency.

Two of George Bush's ▾
children are also in-
volved in politics:
George Walker (left)
became the forty-third
U.S. president in
2001, and Jeb (right)
was elected governor
of Florida in 1998.

Although he lost his bid for reelection in 1992, Bush has had the pleasure of seeing two of his sons follow in his political footsteps. Jeb Bush was elected governor of Florida in 1998, and George W. Bush became the forty-third president of the United States in 2001.

# The Early Years

★ ★ ★

George Herbert Walker Bush was born on June 12, 1924, in Milton, Massachusetts, a suburb of Boston. Bush was the second of five children born to Prescott Sheldon Bush and Dorothy Walker Bush. He was named after his mother's father, George Herbert Walker. Both of Bush's parents had roots in the Midwest. His father was born in Columbus, Ohio. His mother was born in

◄ *Bush's parents, Prescott and Dorothy*

Kennebunkport, Maine, but she was raised in Saint Louis, Missouri.

Prescott Bush worked for the U.S. Rubber Company. He quickly rose through the ranks there. Then he joined a New York investment banking firm where his father-in-law was president.

Soon the Bushes moved to Greenwich, Connecticut, which is a suburb of New York City. There they lived in a large house with a chauffeur, a cook, and a maid. Though young George grew up in a wealthy environment, the Bushes taught their children good values. When the family gathered for breakfast each morning, Bush's father often read from the Bible or prayer books. From his father, who later became a U.S. senator, George learned about duty and service. From

*George Bush at age twelve*

his mother, who raised five children, he learned about the importance of family, love, and discipline.

As a youngster, Bush was nicknamed "Poppy" after his grandfather, who was called "Pop." Bush attended a private grade school in Greenwich. He received a well-rounded education that included Latin, history, geography, and sports.

Every summer, the Bush family spent time at Kennebunkport, where they had a house overlooking the Atlantic Ocean. Bush spent these boyhood vacations swimming, fishing, and boating. Years later, as an adult

◀ Bush grew up spending summers at this house in Kennebunkport, Maine.

and even after he became president, Bush continued to spend time at his Kennebunkport home.

In the autumn of 1937, George entered Phillips Academy in Andover, Massachusetts. His older brother, Prescott Jr., was already a student at this elite school for boys. George quickly became popular with his classmates.

Bush's education was interrupted in the spring of his junior year when he got an infection in his right arm. He was sent to a hospital in Boston. This was before many infection-fighting drugs had been developed. Bush's condition soon became serious. He came close to dying, but he recovered.

*Bush (front center) ▼ was captain of his soccer team at Phillips Academy.*

In the fall of 1941, Bush went back to Andover and completed his studies. He was elected senior class president and became captain of the baseball and soccer teams. George Bush was already proving himself a leader.

On December 7, 1941, while Bush was still in high school, the Japanese attacked Pearl Harbor, Hawaii. The following day, the United States declared war on Japan.

Shortly after he graduated from Phillips Academy in 1942, Bush joined the U.S. Naval Reserve. He took flight training. When he was nineteen, he became the navy's youngest fighter pilot.

During the war, Bush was assigned to an aircraft carrier in the Pacific Ocean. He flew a bomber on many dangerous missions. Then, on September 2, 1944, Bush's plane was hit by enemy gunfire. Bush bailed out over the ocean and was rescued by a U.S. submarine. He was given a medal for his bravery.

▼ *Bush being rescued by a U.S. submarine in the Pacific Ocean during World War II*

Bush returned home to Greenwich on Christmas Eve, 1944. It was a very happy time for the Bush family. Bush's fiancée, Barbara Pierce, was especially glad to see him. George and Barbara were married two weeks later.

*George and Barbara ▶ Bush on their wedding day in 1945*

# Family and Business Matters

★ ★ ★

After World War II ended in August 1945, George and Barbara Bush moved to New Haven, Connecticut. George enrolled at Yale University there and earned top grades. He was elected senior class president and became captain of Yale's championship baseball team.

By that time, the Bushes had a small family. Their first child, George Walker Bush, was

◀ Yale baseball captain George Bush met baseball star Babe Ruth.

George and Barbara ▲
Bush with their first son
and future president,
George Walker

born in July 1946. He would grow up to become governor of Texas and then follow in his father's footsteps as president of the United States.

Bush earned an economics degree from Yale in just 2 1/2 years. He was offered a job in his father's company but decided to strike out on his own. He headed to Texas to get into the oil business.

A family friend gave Bush a job in an oil-equipment company in Odessa, Texas. At that time, the oil business was booming. Bush wanted to get in on the action. In 1950, he quit his job, and he and a friend started their own oil company.

The business quickly became successful, and in 1953, it combined with another firm. Bush and his partners named the new company Zapata Petroleum Corporation. The next year, they started another company, called Zapata Off-Shore Company, to drill for oil in the Gulf of Mexico. Bush was president of this new firm.

But even as Bush's business was growing, his family faced tragedy. Their second child, Robin, had become ill. She was diagnosed with leukemia, an often fatal blood disease. Robin was flown to a New York hospital, where she was treated. Nothing could be done, however. She died at the age of three in 1953. That same year, another son was born to the Bush family. His name was John, although he was nicknamed "Jeb." By 1959, the Bushes had three more children—Neil, Marvin, and Dorothy. By then, the family was living in Houston, Texas.

◄ *George Bush and his family in 1964*

Bush and his ▶
supporters celebrate
a Texas election

Bush's father had been elected a U.S. senator from Connecticut in 1952. This stirred Bush's own interest in politics. Although Texas was a strongly Democratic state, Bush became active in the Republican Party. In 1964, he ran for the U.S. Senate. He campaigned across the state in an attempt to unseat Democratic incumbent Senator Ralph Yarborough.

Though Bush lost the election, it was a close race. This experience only increased Bush's desire to serve in government. In 1966, he quit as president of Zapata Off-Shore company and ran for a seat in the U.S. House of Representatives. This time Bush won. He and his family left Texas for Washington, D.C.

# Mr. Bush Goes to Washington

★  ★  ★

In his first term, Bush was appointed to the powerful House Ways and Means **Committee.** This committee plays a large role in deciding what tax laws are passed. Although Bush was a Republican, he sometimes supported policies favored by Democrats. These included giving eighteen year olds the vote, ending the **draft,** and passing new **civil rights laws.**

He also supported the

◄ George Bush as a member of the U.S. House of Representatives

American soldiers ▲
in Vietnam

Vietnam War, which American troops were then fighting in Southeast Asia. Many Americans thought the United States should not be involved in this war. Protests against the war were widespread. In 1967, Bush traveled to South Vietnam to learn about the war firsthand. He returned home convinced that the United States was on the right path in Vietnam, no matter what the protesters said.

Bush was well liked among Washington's young Republicans. He and Barbara hosted regular Sunday barbecues that made Bush even more popular.

Bush was elected to a second term in Congress in 1968. At the same time, Republican Richard Nixon was elected president. In 1970, Nixon encouraged Bush to give up his House seat and run for the Senate. His opponent

was Democrat
Lloyd Bentsen.
Bush lost the race,
but Nixon reward-
ed him by appoint-
ing him U.S.
ambassador to the
United Nations
(UN). Most coun-
tries in the world
belong to this
organization, which
works to find peaceful solutions to conflicts.

▲ *Lloyd Bentsen*

Many serious international problems are discussed in
the UN. Bush had no experience in **diplomacy** when he
started the job, of course. His experience in business and
politics helped, but he had to learn about diplomacy on
the job.

Bush faced many problems as ambassador to the
UN. One of the most difficult concerned China. In
1949, **communists** had taken over the country. China's
anticommunist leaders escaped to Taiwan, an island off
the southeast coast of China. There they set up a govern-

*Bush served as ▶
ambassador to the
United Nations (UN).*

ment that was admitted to the UN. The communist government of mainland China was not in the UN. Many nations around the world wanted the UN to unseat representatives of the Taiwan government and admit mainland China.

Bush was in a difficult spot. The United States wanted Taiwan to remain in the UN. It also wanted mainland China to join the organization. Bush tried to convince other UN representatives to support the U.S.

position, but they did not. Instead, the UN voted to admit mainland China and throw out Taiwan.

President Richard Nixon was reelected as president in 1972. The following year, Nixon appointed Bush chairman of the Republican National Committee. Soon after, however, Nixon found himself in the middle of a scandal that would end his career.

During the 1972 presidential campaign, people working for Nixon had broken into the Democratic Party headquarters at the Watergate hotel in Washington, D.C. They were looking for information that would help Nixon. Nixon's aides also did many other illegal things in

◄ *Bush as chairman of the Republican National Committee*

their efforts to make sure he would win. When the so-called Watergate scandal came to light, however, Nixon denied being involved.

As chairman of the Republican National Committee (RNC), Bush's most important job was to convince other Republicans to support Nixon. And, as more and more damaging facts were uncovered, he also had to keep up Republican **morale**.

By the summer of 1974, it was clear that Nixon had lied about his involvement in Watergate and in the cover-up that followed. He was losing support in Congress because of the scandal. After

*A newspaper headline ▾ tells of Nixon's 1974 resignation.*

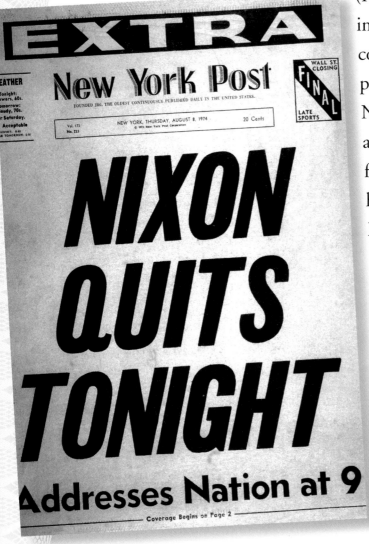

EXTRA

**New York Post**

FOUNDED 1801, THE OLDEST CONTINUOUSLY-PUBLISHED DAILY IN THE UNITED STATES.

WALL ST. CLOSING

FINAL

LATE SPORTS

WEATHER
Tonight:
Showers, 60s.
Tomorrow:
Cloudy, 70s.
For Saturday.
: Acceptable

Vol. 173
No. 223

NEW YORK, THURSDAY, AUGUST 8, 1974.
© 1974 New York Post Corporation

20 Cents

# NIXON QUITS TONIGHT

## Addresses Nation at 9

Coverage Begins on Page 2

discussing the problem
with other Republican
leaders, Bush wrote a letter
to President Nixon. In the
letter he asked Nixon to
leave the presidency.

On August 9, 1974,
Nixon finally quit. This
saddened Bush. He said it
was "not merely a political
disaster, but a human
tragedy."

Vice President Gerald
Ford took over as presi-
dent. He offered Bush his
choice of almost any avail-
able government job.
Although Bush could have

▲ *Richard M. Nixon
after resigning the
presidency*

become the U.S. ambassador in London or Paris, he
chose to go to Beijing, China, instead.

Bush headed the first United States **liaison** office in
China. The office was not an official **embassy,** but Bush
was called an ambassador. One of Bush's tasks in Beijing

*Ambassador George Bush with Chinese politician Lin Ping* ▶

was to promote trade between the United States and China. He also tried to encourage a more friendly relationship between the two countries.

Bush returned to the United States in 1975 when President Ford asked him to become director of the Central Intelligence Agency (CIA). The CIA gathers

information about other countries, often by using spies.
When Bush took over the organization, the CIA was hav-
ing serious problems. Secret information was often leaked
to the press, and Congress was investigating some of the
CIA's past actions. Morale at the agency was very low.
Bush brought his business experience to the agency and
managed to improve the way the CIA was run. He also
improved the morale there.

◄ *George Bush being*
*sworn in as*
*director of the CIA*

# The Path to the Vice Presidency

★ ★ ★

In 1976, Democrat Jimmy Carter was elected president. Like many other Republicans, Bush decided to give up his job in Washington. He and his family went back to Houston.

President Jimmy ▶
Carter and his wife
Rosalynn walked in
the 1977 inaugural
parade.

For Bush, life in Houston was rather quiet after his many years in government. Soon, however, he began doing work for companies that required him to travel far and wide. He visited Australia, China, Denmark, Germany, Egypt, Jordan, and Israel and often took Barbara along. Although Bush once again became successful in business, he was not satisfied. He decided to run for president in 1980.

A group of Bush's supporters started raising money for his campaign. They asked Republicans all over the country to contribute. The many people Bush had met as chairman of the Republican National Committee became very useful.

Bush started campaigning to be the Republican candidate for president three years before the election. He chose James A. Baker to run his campaign. Bush later appointed Baker secretary of state. Bush

▲ *James A. Baker (bottom) ran Bush's presidential campaign.*

gave speeches across the nation supporting Republican candidates. This helped them win elections. One candidate Bush supported was Congressman Dan Quayle of Indiana. He would later serve as Bush's vice president.

Despite all his hard work, Bush lost the race. Instead, the Republicans chose Governor Ronald Reagan of California. A former actor, Reagan was very popular within the Republican Party. Bush's efforts were not in vain, however. Reagan chose Bush to run as his vice president.

In November 1980, Reagan and Bush won a huge victory over President Jimmy Carter and Vice President Walter Mondale. Once again, George and Barbara Bush moved to Washington, D.C. This time they moved into a large home built in 1893 for an admiral. It was the new official house of the U.S. vice president.

Traditionally, vice presidents have few official duties. Their most important job is to cast the deciding vote when there is a tie in the Senate. President Reagan gave Bush many other jobs, however. He asked Bush to lead a number of task forces. One was designed to stop drug smuggling, and another was created to fight terrorism. A third was intended to stop people from entering the United States illegally.

President Reagan and Vice President Bush worked
well together. Bush sometimes disagreed with Reagan's
ideas, but he never said so in public. He gave Reagan his
opinion in private, though. There had long been tensions
between the United States and the Soviet Union, a powerful communist nation. Bush urged Reagan to consider
starting a new series of talks with the Soviet Union aimed
at relieving these tensions.

▲ *President Reagan
(right) and Vice
President Bush*

Bush was vice president for eight years. In that time, he gained valuable experience at the highest levels of government. He visited seventy-five nations around the world, traveled more than 1 million miles (1.6 million kilometers), and talked to many world leaders. He also gained the respect of many Americans. Now he was ready to run for the presidency.

*Reagan (left) ▶ and Bush at work in Washington*

# President George H. W. Bush

★　★　★

George Bush beat Senator Robert Dole of Kansas to become the Republican candidate for president. He chose J. Danforth Quayle III, a forty-one-year-old senator from Indiana, to be his vice presidential running mate.

When Bush became the official Republican candidate

◀ Bush (far right) named Dan Quayle his running mate for the 1988 election.

Bush during his ▶
famous "Read
My Lips" speech

for president, he gave a speech in which he said several things that became important in his campaign. He said he wanted America to be "a kinder, gentler nation." He also promised not to raise taxes saying, "Read my lips: no new taxes." During the campaign, Bush also promised to spend more money on education and to create 30 million new jobs. He said he would cut the number of nuclear missiles in the United States and ask the Soviet Union to reduce theirs, too. He also said he would fight a war on crime and illegal drugs.

The Democratic candidate for president was Governor Michael Dukakis of Massachusetts. His running mate was Lloyd Bentsen, the Texan who had defeated Bush in the Senate race of 1970.

▾ *Democratic candidate Michael Dukakis (left) and running mate Lloyd Bentsen*

Mr. MITCHELL

*Congressional leaders ▲ discuss the Iran-Contra Affair during a 1980 committee hearing.*

Dukakis and Bentsen charged that drug smuggling had increased while Reagan and Bush were in office. They also said that many programs designed to help the needy had been cut. During the campaign, Bush was also accused of knowing about illegal deals to sell arms to Iran, a Middle Eastern nation. The profits from these sales were sent to support rebels, called Contras, in the Central American country of Nicaragua. These strange events were known as the Iran-Contra Affair, and the charges were serious. Early in the race, it seemed likely that Bush would lose the election.

After two televised debates between Bush and Dukakis, however, Bush gained in the polls. President Reagan also helped Bush. The United States had prospered during much of Reagan's years in office. Voters hoped that this would continue under Bush. On Election Day—November 8, 1988—Bush won 426 of 538 electoral votes.

The Bushes moved once again, this time into the White House. First lady Barbara Bush noted that she and George had lived in twenty-eight houses in seventeen cities in forty years. By the time Bush became president, all five Bush children were married and had children of their own. During Bush's presidency, his children and grandchildren visited him often, and they enjoyed many holidays together.

As first lady, Barbara Bush began a nationwide effort to promote **literacy.** She visited more than 500 schools and literacy programs around the country, encouraging people to read. In 1989, she established the Barbara Bush Foundation for Family Literacy, which

Barbara Bush read ▲
to parents and
children as part of
her effort to promote
literacy.

donates money to support these projects. Many Americans admired Barbara Bush for this work. They also liked her smart but simple manner as first lady.

One of the first challenges of Bush's presidency involved the Central American nation of Panama. It was ruled by a **dictator** named Manuel Noriega. He used the Panamanian army to threaten and sometimes kill people who didn't agree with him. He was also involved in drug smuggling. Bush decided to force Noriega from power. In

December 1989, he sent 12,000 troops to Panama. Noriega gave up the next month. He was taken to Florida, where he was tried and convicted for drug dealing. He is still in prison.

Bush's popularity increased after the events in Panama. Before this, some people had called him a "wimp." They said he was not a tough enough leader. Now they thought Bush was strong.

Bush also had to deal with trouble in the Soviet Union. It had been formed in 1922 when Russia and other nations in eastern Europe and central Asia united

◄ *Panamanian dictator Manuel Noriega*

*George Bush (left)* ▲
*and Mikhail
Gorbachev
(far right) discuss
how to reduce
weapons.*

as one country. Now the Soviet Union was facing economic troubles, and it seemed like the country might fall apart. Bush met several times with Soviet leader Mikhail Gorbachev. As a result of these meetings, relations between the United States and the Soviet Union improved. The two countries agreed to reduce their supplies of nuclear weapons.

Bush faced a major crisis in the Middle East in August 1990. Saddam Hussein, the dictator who controlled Iraq, had sent his army into the neighboring country of Kuwait. Kuwait produces one-tenth of the world's oil. It also borders on Saudi Arabia, an important source of oil for the United States. In a nationally televised speech, Bush declared, "This aggression will not stand." He began talking to the leaders of other countries. He wanted them to help the United States force the Iraqis out of Kuwait. The United Kingdom, France, West Germany, Japan, and several Arab countries, including Saudi Arabia, agreed to help the United States in this effort.

▼ *Iraqi president Saddam Hussein*

Bush began sending U.S. military forces to Saudi Arabia. He hoped that this action would convince Iraq to leave Kuwait peacefully. Soon, more than

500,000 U.S. troops were in the area. In November 1990, the United Nations agreed to let the United States and other nations use military force to drive Iraq out of Kuwait if Iraq did not leave by January 15, 1991.

The deadline came, and Iraqi soldiers were still in Kuwait. The next day, Bush ordered bombing raids on Iraqi targets. The Persian Gulf War had begun.

Bush visited ▶ U.S. troops in Saudi Arabia during the Gulf War.

Bombing continued for almost six weeks. Then, on February 23, American troops entered Kuwait and soon defeated the Iraqi army.

After the war, Bush's popularity in the United States soared. Some critics, however, said that American forces had stopped too soon. They said the American troops should have marched into the Iraqi capital of Baghdad

▾ *This scud missile was one of the weapons Iraq used to attack its enemies during the war.*

and forced Saddam Hussein from power. In April, the U.S. military did go into northern Iraq to help a large group of Kurds, an **ethnic minority** who had revolted against the government of Iraq. The United States supplied the Kurds with food, medicine, and military protection.

Bush won praise for the way he handled the crisis in Iraq. At home, however, the United States faced many problems. More than 1,000 savings and loan banks had failed. Many people lost money when they closed. Bush signed a bill to rescue these organizations. The government also needed more money. So in 1990 he signed a bill increasing personal income taxes. Many people were disturbed that he had broken his promise of no new taxes. That same year, he signed the Clean Air Act of 1990. This act set stricter standards for how much pollution could be released into the air.

By December 1991, most of the countries that had been part of the Soviet Union had broken away and declared their independence. Bush quickly established diplomatic relations with these new countries. It was the end of the Soviet Union. The United States was the only truly powerful nation left in the world.

The United States was facing troubling problems, however. There had been a huge oil spill in the sea off the coast of Alaska. Many people were out of work.

▲ *President Bush shook hands with Boris Yeltsin, the first president of Russia, after the break up of the Soviet Union.*

*In 1989, workers tried to clean up after the Exxon Valdez oil spill in Alaska.*

Crime, drug abuse, and homelessness were on the rise. In April 1992, riots broke out in Los Angeles, California, after four policemen accused of beating a black man were found not guilty.

Bush faced reelection that same year. The Democratic candidate for president was the young governor of Arkansas—William Jefferson Clinton. Clinton chose Senator Albert Gore of Tennessee to be his running mate.

It was a difficult campaign for Bush. Even some Republicans were critical of him. Many of them were upset that he had raised taxes when he had promised he would not. Bush's campaign seemed to lack energy and enthusiasm. The Democrats attacked Bush for ignoring the U.S. economy, which had stopped growing.

Voters seemed to want change. They voted for the Clinton-Gore team. Clinton won 43 percent of the popular vote to Bush's 38 percent. An independent candidate, Texas billionaire H. Ross Perot, won about 19 percent of the popular vote. George H. W. Bush's long career in government service would soon be over.

◀ George Bush (left), independent candidate Ross Perot, and Democrat Bill Clinton during a presidential debate

One of Bush's last major actions as president came in December 1992, after he had lost the election. Bush sent American military forces to the African nation of Somalia to help United Nations troops distribute food and other supplies. The Somali people were suffering through a civil war, and many were starving. U.S. help brought relief to that country. Bush said he wanted to end his presidency with this mission of mercy, this "act of idealism."

*Somalis cheered as ◄
U.S. troops arrived
with food and
supplies.*

# The Bush Legacy

★　★　★

**A**fter he lost the election, Bush wrote a note to himself that said, "I hope history will show I did some things right." He believed that among the most important events during his four years as president were the

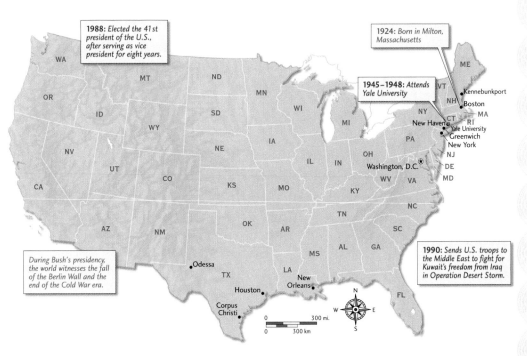

1988: Elected the 41st president of the U.S., after serving as vice president for eight years.

1924: Born in Milton, Massachusetts

1945–1948: Attends Yale University

During Bush's presidency, the world witnesses the fall of the Berlin Wall and the end of the Cold War era.

1990: Sends U.S. troops to the Middle East to fight for Kuwait's freedom from Iraq in Operation Desert Storm.

WA
MT
ND
MN
OR
ID
SD
WI
WY
IA
MI
NV
NE
IL
IN
OH
PA
UT
CO
KS
MO
KY
WV
VA
CA
AZ
NM
OK
AR
TN
NC
MS
AL
GA
SC
TX
LA
FL

Odessa
Houston
Corpus Christi
New Orleans
Washington, D.C.
New Haven
Greenwich
New York
Yale University
Boston
Kennebunkport
ME
VT
NH
NY
CT
RI
MA
NJ
DE
MD

0        300 mi.
0      300 km

N
W    E
S

U.S. victory in the Persian Gulf War and the collapse of the Soviet Union. Bush said that these achievements alone "raised respect for America around the world."

Within the United States, things had not gone so well, however. When Bush left office, the economy was faltering, and many people were out of work. On the plus side, Bush was given credit for solving the savings and loan crisis and passing the Clean Air Act.

*Bush skydiving ▼ to celebrate his seventy-fifth birthday*

Bush has led a productive life since he retired. He has written two books and traveled the world. He seems to be enjoying his role as an elder statesman of U.S. politics.

As he has grown older, Bush has remained active. In 1999, to celebrate his seventy-fifth birthday, George Herbert Walker Bush was skydiving out of an airplane flying at 7,500 feet (2,300 meters).

# GLOSSARY

★ ★ ★

**ambassador**—the representative of a nation's government in another country

**candidate**—someone running for office in an election

**civil rights laws**—laws that make sure that all people are treated equally

**committee**—a group working together on a project

**communists**—followers of an economic system in which all businesses are owned by the government

**dictator**—a government leader in complete control of a country

**diplomacy**—relations between countries

**draft**—a system that chooses people who are compelled by law to serve in the military

**embassy**—a building in one country where the representatives of another country work

**ethnic minority**—people who have different characteristics from the largest groups of people in a country

**liaison**—someone who establishes contact and understanding between two groups

**literacy**—the ability to read and write

**morale**—the feelings of a group or person

# GEORGE HERBERT WALKER BUSH'S LIFE AT A GLANCE

★ ★ ★

## PERSONAL

| | |
|---|---|
| **Nickname:** | Poppy |
| **Birth date:** | June 12, 1924 |
| **Birthplace:** | Milton, Massachusetts |
| **Father's name:** | Prescott Sheldon Bush |
| **Mother's name:** | Dorothy Walker Bush |
| **Education:** | Graduated from Yale University in 1948 |
| **Wife's name:** | Barbara Pierce Bush |
| **Married:** | January 6, 1945 |
| **Children:** | George W. (1946– ); Robin (1949–53); John (1953– ); Neil (1955– ); Marvin (1956– ); Dorothy (1959– ) |

## PUBLIC

| | |
|---|---|
| Occupation before presidency: | Businessman, politician |
| Occupation after presidency: | Retired |
| Military service: | U.S. Navy during World War II |
| Other government positions: | Member of the U.S. House of Representatives from Texas; U.S. ambassador to the United Nations; chairman of the RNC; director of the CIA; vice president of the United States |
| Political party: | Republican |
| Vice president: | J. Danforth "Dan" Quayle III |
| Dates in office: | January 20, 1989–January 20, 1993 |
| Presidential opponent: | Governor Michael S. Dukakis (Democrat), 1988; William Jefferson Clinton (Democrat) and Ross Perot (Independent), 1992 |
| Number of votes (Electoral College): | 48,886,097 of 90,695,171, (426 of 537), 1988; 39,104,545 of 103,756,701, (168 of 538), 1992 |
| Selected Writings: | *Looking Forward* (1987); *A World Transformed* (1998); *All the Best, George Bush: My Life in Letters and Other Writings* (1999) |

★

### George Herbert Walker Bush's Cabinet

Secretary of state:
  James A. Baker, III (1989–1992)
  Lawrence S. Eagleburger (1992–1993)

Secretary of the treasury:
  Nicholas F. Brady (1989–1993)

Secretary of defense:
  Richard Cheney (1989–1993)

Attorney general:
  Dick Thornburgh (1989–1991)
  William P. Barr (1991–1993)

Secretary of the interior:
  Manuel Lujan (1989–1993)

Secretary of agriculture:
  Clayton Yeutter (1989–1991)
  Edward R. Madigan (1991–1993)

Secretary of commerce:
  Robert Mosbacher (1989–1992)
  Barbara H. Franklin (1992–1993)

Secretary of labor:
  Elizabeth H. Dole (1989–1990)
  Lynn Morley Martin (1990–1993)

Secretary of health and human services:
  Louis W. Sullivan (1989–1993)

Secretary of housing and urban development:
  Jack Kemp (1989–1993)

Secretary of transportation:
  Samuel Skinner (1989-91)
  Andrew H. Card (1992–1993)

Secretary of energy:
  James Watkins (1989–1993)

Secretary of education:
  Lauro F. Cavazos Jr. (1989–1991)
  Lamar Alexander (1991–1993)

Secretary of veterans affairs:
  Edward J. Derwinski (1989–1992)

# GEORGE HERBERT WALKER BUSH'S LIFE AND TIMES

★ ★ ★

## BUSH'S LIFE

## WORLD EVENTS

June 12, George Herbert Walker Bush is born in Milton, Massachusetts

**1924**

**1920**

1920    American women get the right to vote

1926    A.A. Milne (above) publishes *Winnie the Pooh*

**1930**

1933    Nazi leader Adolf Hitler is named chancellor of Germany

BUSH'S LIFE

WORLD EVENTS

**1940**

1941   December 7, Japanese
bombers attack Pearl
Harbor, Hawaii
(right), and
America enters
World War II

Joins the U.S. Navy   1942

September 2, Bush's   1944
plane is shot down
over the Pacific Ocean

1944   DNA
(deoxyribonucleic
acid) is found to be
the basis of heredity

January   1945
6, Bush
marries
Barbara
Pierce

July 6,   1946
Bush's first son, George
Walker Bush, is born

Graduates from Yale   1948
University

1949   Birth of the People's
Republic of China

**1950**

February 11, Bush's   1953
son John "Jeb" Bush
is born

1953   The first
Europeans
climb Mount Everest
(above)

55

BUSH'S LIFE

**1960**

WORLD EVENTS

1961   Soviet cosmonaut Yuri Gagarin becomes first person to travel in space

Is elected to the   1966
U.S. House of
Representatives

1968   Civil rights leader Martin Luther King Jr. (right) is shot and killed

**1970**

Is appointed U.S.   1971
ambassador to the
United Nations (below)

1971   Gloria Steinem founds *Ms.* magazine, part of the women's liberation movement of the time

UNITED STATES    UNITED KINGDOM

Is named head of the   1974
U.S. Liaison Office in
Beijing, China

1974   Scientists find that chlorofluorocarbons— chemicals in coolants and propellants—are damaging Earth's ozone layer

Is appointed director   1976
of the Central
Intelligence Agency

1976   U.S. military academies admit women

1978   The first test-tube baby conceived outside its mother's womb is born in Oldham, England

★

## BUSH'S LIFE

Is elected vice 1980
president under
Ronald Reagan

## WORLD EVENTS

**1980**

1983  The AIDS (acquired
immune deficiency
syndrome) virus is
identified

1986  The U.S. space
shuttle *Challenger*
explodes, killing all
seven astronauts on
board

| Presidential Election Results: | | Popular Votes | Electoral Votes |
|---|---|---|---|
| 1988 | George Bush | 48,886,097 | 426 |
| | Michael S. Dukakis | 41,809,074 | 111 |

March, an oil tanker 1989
named the *Exxon
Valdez* crashes near
Valdez, Alaska, spilling
almost 11 million
gallons of crude oil

December, Bush sends
troops to Panama to
overthrow General
Manuel Noriega

1989  On November 9,
enthusiastic Germans
begin tearing down
the Berlin Wall

| BUSH'S LIFE | | WORLD EVENTS | |
|---|---|---|---|

**1990**

August, orders troops to the Persian Gulf after the Iraqi invasion of Kuwait — 1990

1990 Political prisoner Nelson Mandela (below), a leader of the anti-apartheid movement in South Africa, is released. Mandela becomes president of South Africa in 1994.

January 16, the Persian Gulf War begins — 1991

1991 The Soviet Union collapses, and is replaced by the Commonwealth of Independent States

| Presidential Election Results: | | Popular Votes | Electoral Votes |
|---|---|---|---|
| 1992 | William Jefferson Clinton | 44,909,889 | 370 |
| | George H.W. Bush | 39,104,545 | 168 |
| | H. Ross Perot | 19,742,267 | 0 |

December, the United States signs the North American Free Trade Agreement (NAFTA) — 1994

1994 Genocide of 500,000 to 1 million of the minority Tutsi group by rival Hutu people in Rwanda

BUSH'S LIFE

WORLD EVENTS

1996    A sheep is cloned in Scotland

The George Bush Presidential Library opens at Texas A&M University in College Station, Texas    1997

**2000**

Bush's son George Walker Bush is elected president    2000

2000    Draft of the human genome is completed

2001    Terrorist attacks on the two World Trade Center towers in New York City and the Pentagon in Washington, D.C., leave thousands dead

# UNDERSTANDING GEORGE HERBERT WALKER BUSH AND HIS PRESIDENCY

★ ★ ★

## IN THE LIBRARY

Francis, Sandra. *George Bush: The Forty-First President.*
Chanhassen, Minn.: The Child's World, 2001.

Green, Robert. *George Bush: Business Executive and U.S. President.*
Chicago: Ferguson Publishing, 2001.

Joseph, Paul. *George Bush.* Minneapolis: Abdo & Daughters, 2000.

Sufrin, Mark. *The Story of George Bush: The Forty-First President of the United States.* Milwaukee: Gareth Stevens, 1997.

## ON THE WEB

**White House—George Herbert Walker Bush**
*http://www.whitehouse.gov/history/presidents/gb41.html*
To learn more about the life of George H.W. Bush

**Academy of Achievement**
*http://www.achievement.org/autodoc/page/bus0int-1*
To read and see an interview with George H.W. Bush about his life and presidency

**Biography of George Herbert Walker Bush**
*http://bushlibrary.tamu.edu/biographies/president/bio.html*
To read a biography of President George H.W. Bush
illustrated with photographs

**Lieutenant Junior Grade George Bush, USNR**
*http://www.history.navy.mil/faqs/faq10-1.htm*
To read about George H.W. Bush's naval career

## BUSH HISTORIC SITES ACROSS THE COUNTRY

**George Bush Presidential Library and Museum**
1000 George Bush Drive West
College Station, TX 77845
979/260-9552
To view exhibits that highlight the life
and career of President Bush

**George Herbert Walker Bush Birthplace**
173 Adams Street
Milton, MA 02187
To see the house where
President Bush was born

# THE U.S. PRESIDENTS

## *(Years in Office)*

★ ★ ★

1. George Washington
   (March 4, 1789–March 3, 1797)
2. John Adams
   (March 4, 1797–March 3, 1801)
3. Thomas Jefferson
   (March 4, 1801–March 3, 1809)
4. James Madison
   (March 4, 1809–March 3, 1817)
5. James Monroe
   (March 4, 1817–March 3, 1825)
6. John Quincy Adams
   (March 4, 1825–March 3, 1829)
7. Andrew Jackson
   (March 4, 1829–March 3, 1837)
8. Martin Van Buren
   (March 4, 1837–March 3, 1841)
9. William Henry Harrison
   (March 6, 1841–April 4, 1841)
10. John Tyler
    (April 6, 1841–March 3, 1845)
11. James K. Polk
    (March 4, 1845–March 3, 1849)
12. Zachary Taylor
    (March 5, 1849–July 9, 1850)
13. Millard Fillmore
    (July 10, 1850–March 3, 1853)
14. Franklin Pierce
    (March 4, 1853–March 3, 1857)
15. James Buchanan
    (March 4, 1857–March 3, 1861)
16. Abraham Lincoln
    (March 4, 1861–April 15, 1865)
17. Andrew Johnson
    (April 15, 1865–March 3, 1869)

18. Ulysses S. Grant
    (March 4, 1869–March 3, 1877)
19. Rutherford B. Hayes
    (March 4, 1877–March 3, 1881)
20. James Garfield
    (March 4, 1881–Sept 19, 1881)
21. Chester Arthur
    (Sept 20, 1881–March 3, 1885)
22. Grover Cleveland
    (March 4, 1885–March 3, 1889)
23. Benjamin Harrison
    (March 4, 1889–March 3, 1893)
24. Grover Cleveland
    (March 4, 1893–March 3, 1897)
25. William McKinley
    (March 4, 1897–
    September 14, 1901)
26. Theodore Roosevelt
    (September 14, 1901–
    March 3, 1909)
27. William Howard Taft
    (March 4, 1909–March 3, 1913)
28. Woodrow Wilson
    (March 4, 1913–March 3, 1921)
29. Warren G. Harding
    (March 4, 1921–August 2, 1923)
30. Calvin Coolidge
    (August 3, 1923–March 3, 1929)
31. Herbert Hoover
    (March 4, 1929–March 3, 1933)
32. Franklin D. Roosevelt
    (March 4, 1933–April 12, 1945)

33. Harry S. Truman
    (April 12, 1945–
    January 20, 1953)
34. Dwight D. Eisenhower
    (January 20, 1953–
    January 20, 1961)
35. John F. Kennedy
    (January 20, 1961–
    November 22, 1963)
36. Lyndon B. Johnson
    (November 22, 1963–
    January 20, 1969)
37. Richard M. Nixon
    (January 20, 1969–
    August 9, 1974)
38. Gerald R. Ford
    (August 9, 1974–
    January 20, 1977)
39. James Earl Carter
    (January 20, 1977–
    January 20, 1981)
40. Ronald Reagan
    (January 20, 1981–
    January 20, 1989)
41. George H. W. Bush
    (January 20, 1989–
    January 20, 1993)
42. William Jefferson Clinton
    (January 20, 1993–
    January 20, 2001)
43. George W. Bush
    (January 20, 2001– )

# INDEX

★ ★ ★

## ABOUT THE AUTHOR

Marc Davis is a former newspaper reporter, the author of two novels, and a freelance journalist specializing in business, medical, historical, and cultural subjects. His writing and reporting have appeared in national publications and on the Internet. He attended the University of Illinois, Chicago, and New York University. Davis lives in a Chicago suburb.